Racket Down

Brandi Le Ray 5N

Brandi Le Ray 5N

Also available in RED FOX

My Mate Fancies You
Poetry Passions edited by Paul Cookson

Turn that Racket Down

Paul Cookson

Pop-tastic Poetry

A Red Fox Book

Published by Random House Children's Books
20 Vauxhall Bridge Road, London SW1V 2SA

A division of The Random House Group Ltd
London Melbourne Sydney Auckland
Johannesburg and agencies throughout the world

1 3 5 7 9 10 8 6 4 2

First published in Great Britain
by Red Fox, 2001

Printed and bound in Great Britain by
Bookmarque Ltd, Croydon, Surrey

THE RANDOM HOUSE GROUP Limited Reg. No. 954009

ISBN 0 09 941755 3

'Superstar' by Charles Thomson first published in ***Unzip Your Lips***
edited by Paul Cookson, by Macmillan Children's Books 1998

For
Dave, Yvonne, Gregor,
Fraser and Laura

Contents

HOME WORK.

Turn That Racket Down!

Turn that racket down! Are you going deaf?
Turn that racket down! I'm trying to concentrate!
Turn that racket down! Do you call that music?
Turn that racket down! It's making my head ache!

Turn that racket down! I can't hear myself think!
Turn that racket down! It all sounds the same!
Turn that racket down! They can hear it down
the street!
Turn that racket down! It's driving me insane!

I need to get this done!
Can't you see I'm trying to work?
It sends me round the bend!
It's driving me berserk!

Switch that music off right now!
You know it drives me mad!
I need to get my homework done
So . . . TURN THAT RACKET DOWN, DAD!

Paul Cookson

Rock Stars Like They Used to Be

My Granddad's always telling me
Rock Stars aren't what they used to be.

Their hair's too short, their clothes too neat,
They exercise, and don't eat meat.

They don't chase girls, they worship God
Allah, or Buddha or someone odd.

They don't smash guitars, or throw their drums,
They're kind to animals, kids and mums.

They don't swear on telly, or act like stars,
Or drive too fast and crash their cars.

They don't drink or smoke, go wild backstage
They might even live to middle age!

So I've told my Granddad that I agree
That things aren't what they used to be
And when I grow up I'm going to be
A Rock Star like he used to see.

Helen Clare

Right on!

The Record Deal

I've listened to your demo tape
I've come to see your show
And now you want my verdict, boys,
Right then, here we go.

Your singing voice is awful, Baz,
The worst I've heard by far,
Ziggy cannot play the drums
And Og can't play guitar.

The noise you make is dreadful,
Your dress-sense is bizarre
But sign here, lads, you've got a deal,
I think you could go far.

Richard Caley

Cruel Parents!

Dad!
Dad, no!
Dad, please!
Dad, go!
Mum, stop him!
Mum, please!
Mum – NO!
Not you too!
Oh, what shall I do?
You're a cruel, mean, selfish, unfair,
thoughtless, stupid, evil pair!
I disown you as parents for ever more . . .
until you get off that disco floor!

Kate Williams

Kid Rapper

I'm a Year Six rapper, hear what I say
A Year Six rapper, I'll be famous one day
A ten-year-old pop star, doing my thing
Turn on your stereo, hear me sing.

Hey, teacher dude, wanna know what I'm rapping?
Got a rhythm in my brain that my mind keeps
trapping
Make you shake your hips, your finger's snapping
As you prance and dance and your feet start
tapping
That's right, teacher-dude, I'm really happening.

A hot-kid Dee-Jay
try and see it my way
Mr Fame's in town
and I wanna be around
wanna shake his hand
be the biggest in the land
pretty soon you'll see me
rapping on your TV
my wicked bass beat
will knock you off your feet.

Yo, teacher dude, I'm in the playground rapping
Pretty soon from the radio I will be zapping
My hip hop beat and that'll get you slapping
The palms of your hands together, cheering and clapping
Cos I'm the kid rapper, yo I'm really happening.

A Year Six rapper, just you believe me
A ten-year-old pop star, you just wait and see
My name up in lights, fame is the game
When I leave school you'll remember my name
Yo!

David Harmer

Electric Guitars

James Carter

I like electric guitars:
played mellow or moody
frantic or fast – on CDs
or tapes, at home or in
cars – live, in the streets,
at gigs or in bars.
I like
electric
guitars:
played
choppy
like
reggae
or angry
like
rock or
chirpy
like
jazz or
strummy
like
pop or
heavy
like
metal – it
bothers
me not.
I like electric guitars:
their strings and their straps
and their wild wammy bars – their
jangling and twanging and funky
wah-wahs – their fuzz boxes,
frets and multi-effects –
pick-ups, machine
heads, mahogany necks
– their plectrums, their wires,
and big amplifiers. I like electric
guitars: played loudly, politely – dully
or brightly – daily or nightly – badly
or nicely. I like electric guitars:
bass, lead and rhythm –
I basically dig 'em –
I like electric
guitars

Top of the Flops

Ten little pop stars bopping in a line,
One went on a world tour, then there were nine.
Nine little pop stars rapping at the gate,
One joined a reggae band, then there were eight.
Eight little pop stars singing 'Stairway to Heaven',
One appeared on Top of the Flops, then there
were seven.
Seven little pop stars released a dance club mix,
One broke his guitar strings, then there were six.
Six little pop stars performing on stage live,
One got into heavy metal, then there were five.
Five little pop stars chill out on the floor,
One joined a jazz band, then there were four.
Four little pop stars sing 'Baby stay with me',
One became a DJ then there were three.
Three little pop stars rocking at the zoo,
A tiger ate the drumkit, then there were two.
Two little pop stars penned a Euro hit,
One became a heart-throb 'cause he spoke
French a bit.
One little pop star, a guitar in his hand,
His single got to Number 1,
but he's now a one-boy band!

John Rice

Electrifying

rock
shock
damp
amp
switch
glitch
POW!
wow

Mike Johnson

New Dance Crazes About to Sweep the World

When I am a famous pop star
I'm going to create some fantastic new dance
sensations
That will take the world by storm . . .

The elephant with rubber legs
in a strawberry jam swamp shuffle
The drawing pins in my socks
and snake down my vest tango
The tickle your armpits with rhubarb rhumba
The head stuck in a crash helmet shake

The rearrange your pants
without using your hands jive
The all your bones have turned to jelly
and wobbly jaw shiver
The fingers stuck in the ear,
knees glued together sway
The got my braces caught in the kitchen door
in stocking feet on a slippery floor
can't get moving cartoon running on the spot
groove

The best one of all . . .
The can't get that sticky bogey
off the end of my finger linger!

All together now, one two three four . . .
Flick flick shake shake
Flick flick shake shake
Wipe it on the other hand
Flick flick shake shake
Flick flick shake shake
Now it's stuck on both hands
Flick flick both hands
Shake shake both hands
Smear it on the trouser leg
First right then left
Do it once again
Now left then right
Do it once again
All together now, one two three four . . .
Flick flick shake shake . . .

So . . . Bogey on down.

Paul Cookson

Blue Jeans

Doctor, quick! Nurse, the screens!
Dad's got stuck in his old blue jeans.

It's something that comes over him –
that makes him think he's young and slim –

these old songs on the radio
that Mum and Dad both seem to know

(he's a staunch supporter of Status Quo).
But he's got this paunch and he ought to know

if you wear tight jeans it'll all hang out
or get trapped and pinched when you twist and shout.

And we laughed – which only made him worse.
Now he's twisted something. So where's that nurse?

Jill Townsend

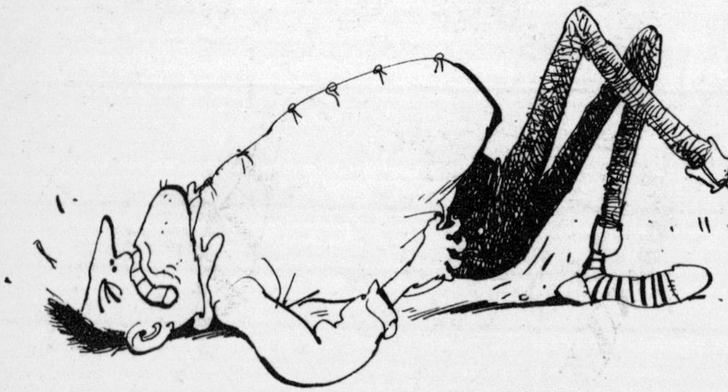

Music Riddle – What Am I?

My first is in **racket** which some say I cause
My second's in **clap** and also **applause**
My third is in **record** and twice can be found
Whilst my fourth is in **cassette** but never in **sound**
My fifth hides in **pop** and also in **song**
My sixth is in **soundtrack** to help you along
My last is in **tune** and **singer** and **stage**
What could I be? I'm now all the rage.

Answer: KARAOKE

Richard Caley

The Destiny Girls

Mum just stood there
At the car boot sale.
Her eyes were watering,
And she was looking upwards

At a vapour trail
Chalking the blue sky.
Dad was holding a flower pot,
One of fifteen,
All different sizes,
For two pounds.

He walked over to Mum,
Clutching the flowerpot;
She held something up to him,
It was an old-fashioned vinyl single.

I walked over to have a look:
It was called 'He Loves Me'
By The Destiny Girls.

Mum was crying,
Still looking up at the vapour trail
Chalking the blue sky,
And I wanted to ask what was happening.

Dad said to me
'She had a beautiful voice, your grandma,

could have been a star. This was her single,
her band, The Destiny Girls, got to about
number 32 . . .'

Dad had never talked about Grandma before.
Mum hadn't either.

She didn't speak now,
Just looked up at the vapour trails
Chalking the blue sky.

'They could have been famous,'
said Dad,
'If they hadn't got on that plane . . .'

Mum said
'At least somebody bought it,
even though it's ended up here,

I'll buy it now, put it with the others.'
He Loves Me
By The Destiny Girls.

Overhead the planes hummed.

Ian McMillan

They Were Great Until

They used to be my favourite band
The greatest group in all the land
Their posters once adorned my wall
Their CDs? I had them all.
I knew their shoe size, heights and weights;
Their favourite foods; their loves; their hates.
I learned the words to every song
But now I see that I was wrong.
They fell from favour on Tuesday night
When Mum said, 'That group's all right.'

Now in my heart is an empty space
Until a new band takes their place.

John Coldwell

Forming a Band

I said,
Let's form a band, okay?
My mate said great –
But what shall we play?
How about Punk?
Boogie-woogie? Hip-hop?
Acid-soul-house-jazz or Pop?
60s, Flower-power, Disco, Soul?
70s influenced? Plain Rock and Roll?
Ambient-pyscho-techno-thrash?
Heavy metal? Hard core? Slash?
80s, Romantics, Garage . . . Shed?

I replied, let's play
With my skateboard instead.

Roger Stevens

A Legend in his Time

Who drives the teeny boppers wild
With his music fast and fab?
Who makes the modern pop-group bands
Seem boring, dull and drab?

Who rocks away ear-splitting nights
With swivelling sexy hips?
Who's got the deepest, darkest eyes
And big thick pouting lips?

Who's the rave of all the girls,
The man who's got the lot?
Is it some young handsome hunk?
IT CERTAINLY IS NOT!

So who's this man who drives 'em wild,
The man who's got it all?
It's the undisputed king of rock –
It's pint-sized Cedric Small.

Five feet tall and sparrow thin,
And eighty six years young,
He plays trombone and piccolo –
And he's only got one lung.

But the thing that really drives 'em wild,
The thing that makes 'em wilt,
Is when he gets his bagpipes out
And plays 'em in his kilt!

They faint and swoon and yell and scream,
Cos everybody sees
The sight they've waited for all night –
His hairy knobbly knees.

And then he grins (he's got no teeth),
And does a Highland fling –
A swirling mass of knees and gums,
The geriatric king.

He swirls, he twirls, he puffs and blows,
He's wild as raging seas,
This toothless, one-lunged pensioner
With hairy, knobbly knees.

So who needs sexy pop-group stars?
Who needs pop-groups at all?
When we've got the best who ever lived
The legend, Cedric Small!

Clive Webster

Loud Music

The walls are all shaking.
The paintwork is flaking.
But why do they blame it on us?
And Dad's belly-aching
Cos windows are breaking.
What is it he wants to discuss?
That Grandma is waking.
The neighbourhood's quaking.
Oh, why does he make such a fuss?

We're moshing. We're rocking.
They may say that's shocking.
But why do they blame it on us?
Now neighbours are flocking.
They're shouting and knocking.
What is it they want to discuss?
Our door needs unlocking.
Their ears need unblocking.
Oh, why do they make such a fuss?

Mum nags and Dad rants on
Like his pants have ants in.
But why do they blame it on us?
And Grandma is prancing
And screeching out: 'Grandson!'
What is it she wants to discuss?
I mean, we're just dancing
To Marilyn Manson.
Oh, why do they make such a . . .
        why do they make such a . . .
                why do they make such a fuss?

Nick Toczek

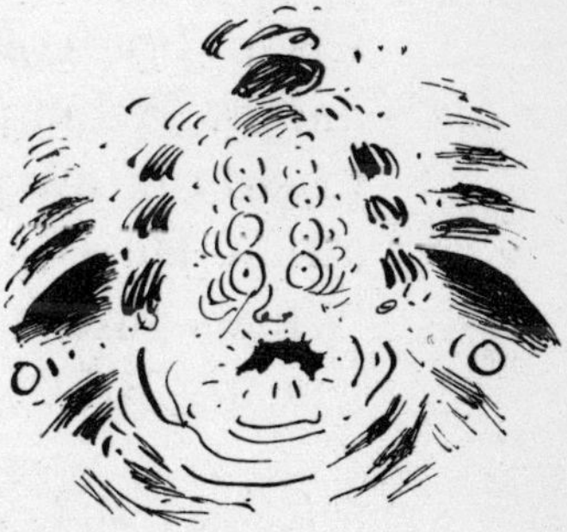

The Day I Nearly Died

After the concert, we waited.
I'd squirmed my way to the front.
Then they came through the door
and the screams and yells
were enough to make anyone deaf.

They were cosmic, ace,
the universal best
but the rest of them
could have been
pop-mag cut outs
the moment his eyes
met mine.

I went hot, cold
and everything in between.
I held out my programme,
a pen. He said:
'What's your name?'
I nearly DIED!

Patricia Leighton

Programme

Superstar

I WANNA BE
A SUPERSTAR
I wanna drive
a massive car
I wanna join
the famous set
I wanna own
a private jet
I wanna lotta
fun at nights
I wanna name
that's up in lights
I wanna lotta
caviar
I WANNA BE
A SUPERSTAR
I wanna have
a lotta fun
I wanna song
at number one
I wanna be
like Dr Who
I wanna be
on TV too
I wannapplause
from near and far

I WANNA BE
A SUPERSTAR
I wanna wear
a lamé suit
I wanna be
a hunky brute
I wanna have
a lotta fun
I wanna headline
in the *Sun*
I wanna fill
the Palladium
I wanna fill
Wembly Stadium
I wanna thrash
a flash guitar
I WANNA BE
A SUPERSTAR!!!

On second thoughts
now let me see . . .
I think I'm better off
as ME!

Charles Thomson

A Pop Pin Up

I pinned the shot of Joey Squall,
mural sized, upon my wall.
He was such a handsome guy
that I could only gaze and sigh.
His ice blue eyes were like twin wells
and exercised a kind of spell.
My love for him was pure and deep
and I drooled till overcome with sleep.
But in the middle of the night,
the pins gave way, the print took flight,
swooping down upon my bed
like a bat, upon my head.
I woke up, smothered, flailing, coughing
and since the night, I've gone right off him.

Marian Swinger

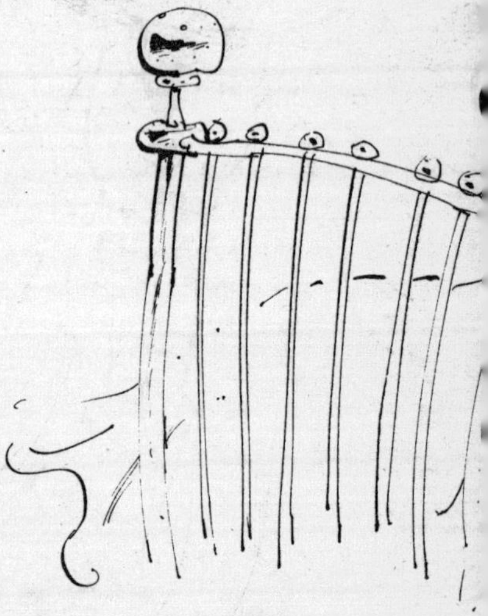

A Noisy Noise Annoys

Lotta gotta
ghetto blaster
gotta lotta
music HOT!

Hear the beat a-
long the street a
treat for some for
others not.

(Hey little lady-o
can you can your radio?

Shan't! Shan't! Shan't!)

Wotta scandal!
Wotta vandal!
Lotta's not a
cat to know!

Wotta brat, an
utter rotter,
nutter with a
radio!

(The hills are alive
with the sound of muzak . . .

I can't stand it
I can't stand it

Lotta the decibel bandit!)

So I gotta
Black biretta
(not a hat a
little gun)

and I shot her
nasty ghetto
blaster wotta
lotta fun!

John Whitworth

Lesley Presley

Grab some earplugs
Get your coat
Lesley Presley is opening her throat

Yeah, Lesley Presley is letting rip
Swivelling her hips
Curling her lip

Note after note
Coming out wrong
Lesley Presley is destroying a song

Our Aunt Lesley
A kindly soul
But not quite the Queen of Rock 'n' Roll!

Bernard Young

All Shook Up

Grandad's got a bottle of Elvis sweat,
He keeps it in a jar in his wardrobe.

He showed it me once, one Summer Sunday;
Just a few drops, glinting in the sun.

'He turned and flicked his hair,' Grandad said,
'one night in Las Vegas, and I happened

to have the jar with me.' Grandad stood up,
holding the jar up like Elvis

might hold a microphone.
'Grandma says it's water from the tap,'

he said, 'but don't you believe her.
This is Elvis sweat. Real Elvis sweat.'

Ian McMillan

What a Racket

Dad shouts, 'What a racket
Turn it down, right away
Sounds like cats being strangled
That's not music, no way!

'The singer can't sing
She's way out of tune
I've heard better in the market
On a wet afternoon

'Where on earth did you get that?
It's worse than bad!'
I said, 'I found it in the attic
In a box marked Dad.'

Roger Stevens

A Bit of a Catch?

When Mum told Dad
she reckoned he was a dead ringer
for the lead singer of a band
she'd seen recently on Top Of The Pops –

same cute face, nice smile, physique, everything! –

he got all proud and pleased as Punch with himself,

at least until he found out
the band she meant
was The Wombles!

Graham Denton

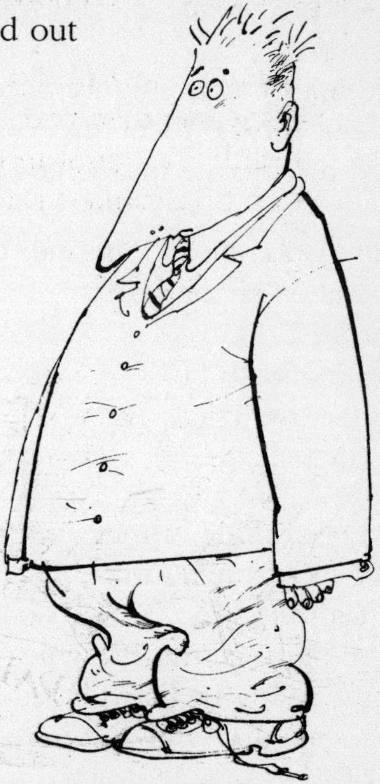

I'm a Hip Hop Tip Top Cool Dude Rapper

I'm a hip hop tip top rappin' cool dude
My beats are kickin' and my words are . . .
a. sofastyoucan'ttellwhati'msayingmymainmanyo
b. rude
c. repetitive
d. *!!!?@%&$*!!
e. Repetitive

I'm a hip hop cool dude rapper, I'm top
I rap and I rap till I just can't . . .
a. get my breath
b. stop
c. think of anything else to say
d. wait for the toilet any longer and the beat
   is driving me insane cos it all sounds the same

A hip hop cool dude rapper that's me
Remember my name . . .
a. E ZEE 2 C
b. Skegness On C
c. Batter C Dog's Home
d. Chel C Nil

I'm a cool dude rapper, misunderstood
And I like to hang out . . .
a. with the boyz 'n the 'hood
b. the girls in the Brownies
c. the teddy bears who are having their
   picnic if you go down to the wood
d. of trees upside down

I'm a cool dude rapper, I'm king of the mike
I'm the big boss man and I do . . .
a. what my mum tells me to do
b. big burps into the microphone
c. what I like
d. nothing

I'm a tip top hip hop rapper and I'm
Always in time and my wurdz all . . .
a. sound exactly the same
b. rhyme all the time and it ain't no crime cos it sounds just fine with the bump and grind and the rhythm you find is mine all mine line after line, rhyme after rhyme
c. sound like nursery rhymes
d. aren't mine cos I'm just rappin' an old song in a new way cos I can't think of nuthin new

Paul Cookson

Pavarotti Notti

The loudest noise in the whole wide world,
The 'orriblest of dins,
Is when my dad gets in the bath –
He just lies there and . . . SINGS!

He doesn't bother getting washed,
And boring stuff like that –
He just lies there and lets it rip
Like a squawking strangled cat.

And yet he thinks he sounds superb,
He thinks he's Pavarotti –
He's more like a pig with belly-ache,
He's driving us all potty.

I reckon with his mighty lungs
He'd not have any trouble
Blasting through a block of flats
And raising 'em to rubble.

Or standing there on Blackpool Beach
With mighty lungs gigantic
And being heard with ease sublime
Across the wide Atlantic.

He could also contact aliens
By yelling up through space,
No need for rocket ships and such –
Just the hole in Father's face.

So when you talk of noise and dins,
The 'orriblest of all
Is the din we suffer at our house –
It's Father's bathroom bawl!

Clive Webster

Musical Musing

Just for once
I'd love to hear it –
music to the ear –

Mother shouting,
(Turn that racket
UP
so I can hear!)

Graham Denton

Popstar kit:

Contains:
Squeaky voice box
Stick on goatee beard/blond hairdo
Snake hips (one size fits all)
Baggy show-your-bottom skateboard trousers
Back to front baseball cap
Pair of pouty lips
Peel-on peel-off sneer.
Cassette tape of terrible songs
Handful of tenners to bribe friends to scream at you.
Sunglasses for your dad to wear
(so you can pretend he's your minder).

Warning! This kit may not work if you
are at all talented in any way.

Diana Velia

School Disco. 'And here is An Oldie, Especially For The Teachers'

Mr Hepps steps like a spaceman
walking on the moon.
Miss Smithers quivers like blancmange
whacked with a wooden spoon.
Miss Grounds bounds across the floor
like a cheeky kangaroo.
Mr Phipps skips like a boy,
busting for the loo.
Miss Serks jerks like someone's dropped
a spider down her back.
Miss Fitches twitches like a batch
of bunnies in a sack.
Mr Searles twirls round and round
like a windmill in a gale.
Mrs Jacques shakes her foot
like she's caught it in a pail.

They're working so hard to look hip and cool
But they need to spend time at a dancing school.

John Coldwell

The Voice

Mirrors cracked and tumblers shattered,
puppies howled and children scattered,
hamsters fainted, babies cried,
fleas left cats and budgies died,
ornaments fell off the shelves,
frightened toddlers wet themselves,
passers-by stopped dead and shivered,
visitors grew pale and quivered,
headaches blossomed, eardrums rang
whenever Cousin Katie sang.
She's weakened several ailing hearts
but now her CD's in the charts,
sold in every CD shop
and climbing to the very top,
soon to be the number one.
Still, we hear that voice and run!

Marian Swinger

Gyration Gap

'*Listen*! That's *music* to my ears!'
Sighed Dad, when my CD ended.

So I put the CD on again –
Which was *not* what he'd intended . . .!

Trevor Harvey

The Group

There wasn't much to do today
so Malcolm and me and Ian Gray
planned how we might form a group
with me on keyboards, Malcolm on drums
and Ian who knew how to strum a C
or a G on his brother's guitar.

Then Ian's sister came waltzing in
with her friend Sharon and wanted to know
why they couldn't be in the group as well
and when we said no, they threatened to tell
some dreadful secret and Ian turned white,
said they could stay if they kept really quiet.

Then we argued a bit about the name
'The Werewolves' I said or 'The Sewer Rats'
or 'The Anti Everything Parents Say'
but Malc said no, it ought to be simple
and Ian said maybe 'The group with no name'
while his sister and Sharon said something silly
and Malcolm and I ignored them completely

And I thought we ought to write some songs,
'Easy,' we said, 'it wouldn't take long
to knock off another Hold onto your love,

don't let her go, oh no, no, no!
And Malc kept the beat with slaps on his knee
while I played kazoo or a paper and comb
till Sharon yawned, then got up and went home.

Then Ian's sister and Ian sat down
while we stood around and said what to write,
and it sounded all right till we tried it out
and discovered how awful it was
'Let's knock it on the head,' I said,
'we'll need another year or two
before we get it right.'

And later that night on the short walk home
I said to Malc that I thought we ought
to dump the others and go it alone.
We should have seen it all along,
two good-looking dudes like us,
we'd be famous in no time.

But Malc said we were overlooking
one small but very important thing:
Neither of us could sing!

Brian Moses

Famous Fan

I'm an ordinary person
but I wrote to a famous person recently.
First time I've ever done that.
I wrote to tell him how much
I enjoyed his music.
I felt so stupid afterwards –
lots of people must write to tell him that.

But guess what?
He replied!
I was so surprised
and now I feel really great
because even though
I'm still an ordinary person
my favourite pop star's heard of me!

Philip Waddell

Got the Beat
(A poem to chant out loud and dance to)

Got the beat. . . . . .Got the beat

Got the beat got the beat got the beat
Repeat
Got the beat. . . . . .Got the beat

Got the beat got the beat got the beat
Repeat
Got the beat Waah!
Got the beat Wooh!
Got the beat got the beat got the beat
Repeat
Got the beat Waah! Chugga chugga chugga
Got the beat Whooh! Vumm Vumm
Got the beat got the beat got the beat
Repeat
Slow down
Beat
Beat
Slow down
Beat
Beat
Speed up beat beat be be be be beat
Speed up beat beat be be be be beat
I said groove baby got the beat
I said move baby got the beat

Got the beat got the beat gotta move your feet
Got the beat got the beat gotta feel the heat
Got the beat got the beat gotta keep it neat
Got the beat got the beat gotta leave your seat
Gotta keep it neat gotta feel the heat
Gotta move your feet gotta feel the beat
I said groove baby got the beat
I said move baby got the beat
Dum dum

Gotta feel the beat

Dum dum

Gotta feel the beat

Got the beat

Got the beat

Got the beat got the beat got the beat
Complete

Paul Cookson

Hey You, Be a Heavy Rock Star

1) Got your band together but it needs a name, is it:
a) The Cuddly Cuties?
b) The Four Fine Fellows?
c) Heavy Gothrock Street of Shame?

2) Your very first CD's out today, is it called:
a) I'll Never Forget the Tears I cried the Day I Lost my Fluffy Panda?
b) May I Go to the Pictures With You Tomorrow or If Not, Perhaps Next Saturday?
c) The Hulking Braindead Zombie's Birthday?

3) Which new image suits you best, is it:
a) Yellow tutu, platform shoes and a purple top hat covered in mirrors?
b) School blazers with a very smart stripy tie?
c) Leather jeans, chains and a hairy chest?

4) Making your video was very hard:
a) Because it was set backstage in Nellie Nugget's Dancing School?
b) Because it was set in the school playground?
c) Because it was set under three tons of old rusty cars and four Rottweilers in a massive scrapyard?

5) When you play live gigs your favourite trick is to:
a) Get the crowd to skip round the stadium, holding hands and waving flowers?
b) Ask everyone to join in with some rather super choral singing?
c) Body surf the mosh pit, spit on the sweaty fans and then be sick?

David Harmer

My Mate Fancies You!

Paul Cookson

I was only a wee little sprog
When I had my very first snog
Ten minutes long
All dribbles and tongue . . .
It's a pity it was from my dog!

Ever banged noses on your first snog? Or been dumped after only a day? Could you spot a brother or sister in love? Then open up this hilarious collection of tonsil-tickling passion poems chosen by Paul Cookson.

You'll love it!

£2.99 009940964X

Swings and Shadows

Edited by Anne Harvey

This rich collection of poetry celebrates the many moods and experiences, the swings and shadows, of childhood. Tracing her own growing up years, Anne Harvey, the acclaimed anthologist, has chosen widely from the excitingly new to the classic half-remembered favourite. Readers of all ages will find something to their taste.

'As a child I would rather have been starved of food than poetry. Swings and Shadows is an excellent anthology.'
Anne Fine

£5.99 0099646811

The Naughtiest Children I Know

Edited by Anne Harvey

My son Augustus, in the street, one day,
Was feeling quite exceptionally merry.
A stranger asked him: 'Can you show me, pray,
The quickest way to Brompton Cemetery?'
'The quickest way? You bet I can!' said Gus,
And pushed the fellow underneath a bus.

Whatever people say about my son,
He does enjoy his little bit of fun.

An A-Z of the naughtiest children ever! From untidy Amanda and Bad Boy Benjamin to Naughty Dan, Greedy George and Sulky Susan. They're all inside, so open up and see if there's a poem in here about you…

£5.99 009940866X

RATUS POCHE

COLLECTION DIRIGÉE PAR JEANINE ET JEAN GUION

Tico fait du vélo

 ISSN 1259 4652, ISBN 2-218 05564-3

La tarte de Métal

suivie de

Tico fait du vélo

Deux histoires de Jeanine et Jean Guion
illustrées par Pierre Cornuel

HATIER

Métal, le robot, est le plus fort.

LES PERSONNAGES DES HISTOIRES

Tico est très malin.

Plumet aime les câlins.

Où est le bon dessin ?

La tarte de Métal

Plumet est dans le salon. 1

Métal est dans la cuisine. 2

Le robot fait une tarte 3
pour son ami Plumet.

Où est la tarte de Métal ?

– La tarte est finie,

dit Métal.

C’est une tarte

aux pommes. 4

Que veut ajouter Plumet sur sa tarte ?

– Je veux ajouter 5

du sucre, dit Plumet. 6

Et il va

dans la cuisine.

Que dit Plumet dans l'histoire ?

(10)

(11)

(12)

(13)

Plumet est revenu

dans le salon.

Il avale une bouchée 7

de tarte.

– Pouah ! dit Plumet.

C'est salé !

Qui a mis le sel dans le pot à sucre ?

14

15

– Oh ! dit Métal,
j'ai oublié 8
de te dire que
j'avais mis le sel 9
dans le pot à sucre. 10

FIN

Où est le bon dessin ?

Tico fait du vélo

Tico roule sur son joli vélo.

Métal regarde son ami.

Tico dit au robot :

– Monte sur mon vélo,

je te le prête. 11

Mais Métal est lourd

et le vélo se casse !

Que fait Métal, dans l'histoire ?

4

5

6

Métal est désolé. 12

Il dit à Tico :

– J'ai cassé

ton joli vélo.

Je vais aller le réparer 13

dans mon atelier. 14

Dans l'histoire, que font Tico et Plumet ?

Métal est de retour.

Il a tout réparé.

Tico monte sur le vélo.

Plumet saute

dans la sacoche.

Tico pédale fort.

Plumet crie :

– Plus vite ! Plus vite !

Qu'arrive-t-il au vélo dans l'histoire ?

Tout à coup, le vélo
se met à siffler 16
et à rouler si vite
que les roues 17
ne touchent plus le sol ! 18
– Au secours ! crie Plumet.
On va trop vite !

Où est le bon dessin ?

13

14

15

Le vélo s'arrête devant Métal. 19

– Il ne faut pas avoir peur, 20

dit le robot.

J'ai juste ajouté

deux petits moteurs

télécommandés. 21

J'avais oublié de le dire à Tico !

Métal a inventé le vélo-fusée !

FIN

alphabet des **majuscules**

A – a	**H – h**	**O – o**	**V – v**
B – b	**I – i**	**P – p**	**W – w**
C – c	**J – j**	**Q – q**	**X – x**
D – d	**K – k**	**R – r**	**Y – y**
E – e	**L – l**	**S – s**	**Z – z**
F – f	**M – m**	**T – t**	
G – g	**N – n**	**U – u**	

1

un **salon**

2

une **cuisine**

3

une **tarte**

4

une **pomme**

5

ajouter *(a-jou-té)*

Il **ajoute** du sucre.

6

un **sucre**

7

une **bouchée**

Ce qui va dans la bouche.

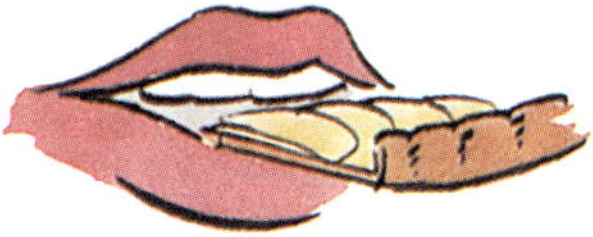

8

oublié

Il a **oublié** son sac.

9

le **sel**

Le **sel** est salé.

10

un **pot**

11

je **prête**

Elle **prête** sa poupée.

12

désolé

Il est **désolé.**

13

aller *(a-lé)*

réparer *(ré-pa-ré)*

14

un **atelier** *(a-te-li.é)*

15

il **saute**

16

il se **met** *(mè)*
à **siffler** *(si-flé)*

17

les **roues** *(rou)*

18

touchent *(touch)*

19

devant
Elle est **devant.**

20

faut *(fo)*

peur
Il a **peur.**

21

télécommandés
Des moteurs que l'on fait marcher de loin.